The us 4
Ever Club

The Us 4 Ever Club

Ever Club

When a Friend Has More

By Joann Klusmeyer
Illustrated by Betty Wind

Publishing House
St. Louis

Copyright © 1987 Concordia Publishing House
3558 S. Jefferson Avenue, St. Louis, MO 63118-3968
Manufactured in the United States of America

Library of Congress Cataloging-in-Publication Data

Klusmeyer, Joann, 1933–
    The Us 4 Ever Club.

        Summary: Phyl asks the Lord for help in curbing her jealousy towards a rich, pampered, musically talented member of the Us 4 Ever Club.
        [1. Clubs—Fiction.   2. Friendship—Fiction.   3. Jealousy—Fiction.   4. Christian life—Fiction]
I. Title.   II. Title: Us Four Ever Club.   III. Title: Us for Ever Club.
PZ7.K688Us   1987   [Fic]   87-900
ISBN 0-570-03644-5

1 2 3 4 5 6 7 8 9 10 DB 96 95 94 93 92 91 90 89 88 87

To Jason, Matthew, Daniel, and
Bethany Anne,
four of my favorite people

Contents

1
The Us 4 Ever Club

"Just think, it's getting to be that time again," said Phyllis, generally known as Phyl. The other three girls in the clubhouse nodded and looked at her thoughtfully.

Marty sat on the table swinging her bare feet and wiggling her toes. "Instead of 'The Seventh Grade Club,' maybe we should change the name of the club to 'The Us 4 Ever Club.' And make the 'four' the number 4 instead of f-o-r or f-o-u-r. Get it? It sounds like 'Us, forever,' but we'd know it really means 'Us four, ever a club.' Not only that, but we'd never have to change our name ever again."

Pat, whose feet kept time with Marty's, agreed. "Hey, yeah; that's a neat name!"

Phyl was stretched out on the floor beneath the swinging feet. She reached over to the broom leaning against the nearby wall and pulled a straw to nibble, but thought of a more interesting thing to do. She dragged the coarse straw across the bottom of the nearest foot.

"EEEK!" Marty's squeal shook the clubhouse walls. "Cut that out! You know I have ticklish feet!"

"Doesn't everyone?" asked Phyl as she broke the straw in one-inch pieces.

The fourth member of the group brushed her long, blond hair while she stared at the ceiling. Andrea (Andy) was required to brush her hair 100 strokes each day—"one of my mother's weird ideas"—so she often did her brushing during the club meetings.

"Penny for your thought, Andy. Or has inflation hit them too? Sorry, but a penny is about all I can afford."

"Actually, money was on my mind—sort of,"

Andy answered. "This clubhouse needs something done to it. It looks like it was made for grade schoolers."

"It was," Phyl reminded her.

"But not after next week—unless one of us flunks," Andrea pointed out.

"How about a coat of paint on the walls?" suggested Pat. "Maybe two coats," she added as her gaze wandered about the walls. "Remember how hard it was to hide the crayon marks last time?"

"Yeah," agreed Andy. "Maybe paint for the furniture, too."

The clubhouse had been built six years ago when the girls were in the first grade. They had known each other since Kindergarten, but had officially formed the club in first grade.

They were walking home from school together when the idea first hit. The yellow and brown leaves were falling on the sidewalk and the girls were running through them, scuffling their feet to send the leaves flying.

"Let's make a club," Pat suggested, " . . . with four members. We can have our meetings walking home from school."

11

By the time they reached the first house, Phyl's, they were deciding on a name. "How about 'Elm Street Club'?" one of them suggested. "We always walk home this way, and we all live here."

The girls looked at each other, but Andrea's head drooped. "I'm going to move next week."

"Move? You can't. You're already in the club."

"I have to," Andy whined. "My daddy said so. He said this house is too small. We have to have a big house with a big room for me, 'cause he's gonna buy me a piano."

The news exploded the tower of plans the girls had been building. Then practical Marty asked, "Where are you moving?"

"Over to Poplar Street. See right through the trees there? You can see the roof."

"Andy! You were teasing us! We can still be a club; we just have to think up a different name."

"How about 'The First Grade Club'?" suggested Phyl. "That would fit everyone."

"That's a good name," agreed the girls, and they called good-byes as they walked on.

Phyl waved and dashed into her house. "Mother!" she called. When she located her mother preparing supper, she asked the question. "Andy's moving to a bigger house so she can have a piano; can I have one, too?"

Her mother's silence told Phyl what she dreaded to hear. There would be no bigger house and no piano, either. There were brothers and sisters, older and younger. There were plans for a new baby about to be born. A bigger house was needed, but not being planned.

Later that evening Phyl asked her mother, "Why does God give everything to some people, but not us? It doesn't seem fair."

Mother replied, "You're still thinking about Andrea's piano, aren't you? Tell me, does she have brothers and sisters?" Phyl shook her head. Mother continued, "We all have good things, but perhaps not the same good things. God gave you a family."

Phyl looked around the room. Her oldest brother and sister, twins, were stretched out on the floor watching TV. The next brother, just barely older than Phyl, was also on the floor, trying to unravel the mysteries of multiplication. Phyl was sitting on the floor by her mother's chair, resting her head against her mother's knee. In one corner sat another brother and sister, twins again, playing with a new set of blocks. They would start Kindergarten next year.

And then there would be the new baby. Seven, no matter how many times they were counted— unless the baby would be twins again. The living room floor was covered with children.

Phyl's father entered the room and walked through, picking his way among the children. Phyl shut her eyes and tried to imagine herself alone in the room, but it was impossible. She had no memory of being home alone, so there was nothing to remember.

That evening was the first of many times Phyl noticed that there were certain things that people with large families could not have. Were brothers and sisters worth it?

On the day The First Grade Club was formed, the remaining three members skipped down Elm Street, still making the leaves fly before their feet.

"Is it a really, truly big piano? Not a toy?" Marty asked. "Do you really want one?"

"I don't know," Andy hesitated. "No one asked me if I wanted it. My mother said six was the age to learn, so she found me a teacher."

"I think it'll be fun. We can come over to your new house and sing while you play."

Andy's uncertainty melted under Marty's confident reassurance.

"Hey, just think!" put in Pat. "When you get big, you can play the piano at church. Maybe you'll even give concerts at the stadium or wherever people give concerts."

"I don't think it's the stadium; I think they play ball there," Marty advised.

"Well, it's some big place," insisted Pat. "Andy will be dressed up in a long dress with feathers and sequins, and have lots of rings on her fingers, and she'll play music for presidents and maybe even kings." Shy Andy wished she would never see a piano. The thought of playing in public scared the six-year-old.

When they reached Marty's house, she darted through the gate and dashed up the walk to her house. "See you in the morning," she called.

Pat and Andy walked on, deep in thought. After a block, Andy voiced her fear. "I don't think I want a piano."

"Sure you do," Pat assured her. "It'll be fun—

like Marty said. We'll sing with you. I'm gonna like that."

Andy didn't reply. Instead, she wondered why Pat wasn't afraid of things the way she was. Maybe because Pat had big brothers—lots of them. Some were old enough to drive, and the yard was full of cars all the time. Her brothers didn't pay much attention to Pat, but they were always around— so Pat didn't have to have a sitter when her parents weren't home. Most of Andy's sitters were strangers, and sometimes they didn't like kids anyway. Andy knew a lot about sitters.

Well, she thought, if Marty and Pat stick with me, things might be a little brighter. If I play the piano, I won't be so lonely. I'll just have to tell people that I don't want to play a concert and wear a fancy dress and lots of rings. No one can make me play a concert . . . can they?

After Pat parted at her house, Andy continued on alone. As she entered her yard, she saw her mother's car turn into the driveway.

Good. Maybe Mom will be home tonight, and we can talk about the piano. And I'll tell her about The First Grade Club. And I'll tell her that Phyl's new baby might be twins. The doctor said so, and doctors know stuff like that.

The excitement tickled Andy's feet, and she broke into a run to greet her mom.

"Don't run, Andrea; you might fall," her mother called. Andy slowed to a walk while her mother waited for her.

Mother put her arm around Andy's shoulder and walked with her to the front door. "And how was your day?" Mom asked.

"Good! I have lots of stuff to tell you. You're not leaving again, are you?"

"Not for a little while. I do have a meeting, but you can tell me all those things while I get ready."

Disappointment tugged at the smile on Andy's lips, but she held it there. She had lots of practice at hiding disappointment. At least she had a little while with her mother—and she wasn't going to spoil it by crying. Mom does many important things, Andy told herself, and I have no right to cry just because I'm lonely.

Andy's father, too, was away from home often—sometimes several days or a week at a time. He always brought Andy a gift when he returned,

17

but sometimes she wished he were not so important. Then he would be home more.

Andy opened the door for her mother and waited for her to enter. "Thank you, Darling," her mother said with a smile.

Andy remembered to return the smile and say, "You're welcome." Mother liked smiles and politeness and things like that, and Andy wanted her mother to like her.

"Mother, do people go to big buildings and play concerts for important people?" Andy asked.

"Sometimes," her mother replied, " . . . if they are good enough. Is that what you want to do?"

"I . . . I don't know."

"Always remember, Andrea, with God's help you can do what you really want to, if you're willing to work very hard. Will you always remember that?"

Andy nodded. "Guess what? Phyl's new baby might be twins! The doctor said so."

"You mean, Phyl's *mother's* new baby," Mother corrected. "How many children will that make?"

Andy's eyes were shining with excitement.

18

"Eight, if it's twins. Seven, if it isn't. I hope it's twins."

Andy's mother shook her head slowly as she went to the closet for a dress.

"I joined a club today," Andy told her mother.

"You did?"

Since Mother didn't ask what club it was, Andy told her. "It's The First Grade Club, and the other members are Phyl, Marty, and Pat."

"That sounds like a very nice club. When we move to the new house, perhaps your father will have a clubhouse built for you."

Andy's eyes widened with excitement, and the wonderful thought hit her like a thunderbolt. If she had the clubhouse in her yard, the other girls would come to see her a lot. It would be almost like having sisters. "Do you really think he will? Could it have tables and chairs and a TV and a big bookcase? Do you think he really will?"

"I'm sure he will, Darling. Run along, now, and open the door. That must be the lady who will be staying with you this evening."

Andy went to the door, but she did not hurry. The arrival of the sitter meant the departure of her mother. But this time it would not be all bad.

Andy had a great big beautiful thought to keep her company. Andy appreciated exciting thoughts. She could lie in bed and think about them and not be so lonely. She could even pretend-believe Father and Mother were not away.

This had been the day the club's long friendship had begun. The next September the club was forced to change its name to The Second Grade Club.

Andy's piano affected the club more than the girls had suspected. None of the four had known how much practice was required to play the piano. Many afternoons three girls sat in the clubhouse while another very unhappy girl practiced her scales. After a few months Andrea tried setting her alarm clock an hour early so she could get her practice over with and play in the afternoon, but it didn't work. She was so sleepy before breakfast that she couldn't keep her fingers moving.

Many afternoons that year Andy persuaded the others to wait in her room while she finished. Phyl would sit on the bench with Andy and turn the pages. Pat and Marty would read Andy's books

or play with her dolls. Andy thought that was better than being alone.

The following year The Third Grade Club performed in a school talent show. Andy played and
the others sang a three-part round about trains
pulling out of a station. Although Andy thought
her fingers would turn to icicles, she felt lucky—
she didn't have to sing, and she could sit with her
back to the audience. They won the Junior Level
prize, so the next time they performed was easier.

By the time they called themselves The Fifth
Grade Club, the quartet had made a local name
for itself. Andy had even found the courage to sing
with the others.

Now they were ending sixth grade and re-
naming themselves The Us 4 Ever Club.

"Ninety-seven, ninety-eight, ninety-nine, one
hundred!" counted Andy and slid the hair brush
across the table.

"You missed one," teased Marty. "I distinctly
heard you forget 56."

"How can you hear someone forget?" challenged Pat. "Besides, it was 55, not 56."

Andy smiled and said nothing . . . not after six years of teasing about her mother's many rules.

"What color do you think it ought to be?" asked Phyl.

"What color do you think what should be," asked Pat, "the 55 or the 56?"

"You don't color numbers, you nut. You taste numbers. I'm starving; I haven't had supper yet, and it's almost seven."

"I'll get some sandwiches," offered Andy. "What kind would you like?" She always asked, knowing the vote would be for peanut butter and jelly.

"Make mine hummingbird's tongues," requested Marty, "with peanut butter and jelly, of course."

"I think it ought to be green," insisted Phyl.

"Who ever heard of a green-hummingbird-tongue peanut butter and jelly sandwich?" puzzled Marty.

Andy left for the sandwiches.

Phyl turned the conversation back to redecorating the clubhouse. "Don't you think green would be pretty?"

"Green's okay, but I like other colors, too."

Marty nodded. "If we use green, then we'll have to paint the furniture too."

"That wouldn't take very long," pointed out Phyl.

After a minute of silence Pat said, "You know what I think? We need a cassette recorder."

"A recorder!" echoed Phyl and Marty together. "What for?"

"I think we need to know exactly how our quartet sounds. We could listen to ourselves and fix our mistakes."

"Hey, that's a good idea," agreed Marty. "What do you think, Phyl?"

"Sounds good. Maybe we could do the painting and get that, too."

The door opened. "Get what too?" asked Andy from behind a mound of sandwiches.

"Pat thought we need a cassette recorder so we could hear ourselves sing."

"Hey, yes. That's a good idea."

"I have a question," Marty stated abruptly as she raised her hand. When she had their attention, she lowered her hand. "Have any ideas on what we use for money?"

"Why did you have to go and bring up that?" complained Pat. "I could almost hear the haunting strains of melody we would record."

Marty cupped her hand behind her ear. "That haunting strain you hear is probably my mother calling me. I promised to babysit with Gwennie tonight. Gwennie—I just love that name. She even gets two nice names—Gwendolyn Annette. But me? I was born 10 years too soon, and look—Martha Lou. When I get to be president, I'm going to make a law against naming kids after great-aunts."

"When you get to be president, I'm going to find a new country," Phyl stated flatly.

Marty stuck out her tongue in the general direction of Phyl and reached for the doorknob. As she bowed ceremoniously, she assured them, "Parting is such sweet sorrow; so, until we meet again . . ."

"Shut the door," yelled Pat, " . . . from the outside."

"You really know how to hurt," declared

24

Marty. "First they name me Martha Lou, and then you insult me."

"Good-bye!" insisted Pat as the door closed behind Marty.

Phyl's nimble toes picked up a pencil from the floor and moved it in the general direction of Pat. Pat took it and handed it, along with an empty envelope, to Andy. "Now you're ready."

"Ready for what?"

"We're going to think of ways to become millionaires in the next month. You can write them down."

Andy took the envelope and pencil and began to write. When she finished, Pat asked, "What did you write?"

"I have the list already made," Andy told them. "I'll read it to you. 'Number One, find an oil well. Number Two, invest in a hit movie. Number Three, play the stock market. Number Four, buy real estate.' "

"C'mon," Phyl urged. "Be real!"

"Hey, how about lawn mowing?" Pat asked enthusiastically. "Think we could do it? There's lots of grass over summer."

"What would we do for a mower?" Phyl pointed out.

"I think I could get one," offered Andy.

"I'll bet you could," retorted Phyl. "You seem to be able to get anything."

"I only meant, I think we could use ours. It just stays in the garage all the time."

"Because you have a gardener, now?"

Andy said nothing. Phyl could get catty at times.

Pat looked from one to the other, then announced, "Meeting adjourned. The mowing sounds good to me, but let's each do some thinking. Maybe someone will have a brainstorm. Okay?"

Andy nodded, and Phyl and Pat left the clubhouse.

The sun had set and shadows were tall across the street. The girls walked in silence till they reached Pat's house. After a good-bye, Phyl walked on alone.

Why do I do it? Phil asked herself. There is no reason to say the things I said. There is no reason, but I said them anyway. Andy can't help it that she can have anything she wants—like her own room, the clubhouse in her back yard, and that big beautiful piano. This is even her second one! The one she got in first grade isn't good enough anymore. The new one takes up almost half her room. Why can't I be happy for her? Dear God, why do I do it? You know I love You and try hard to be like You. Why do You let me do it?

The question hung answerless in the air as Phyl reached her front door. She could hear the TV before she entered. Laughter sounded from an upstairs room. In the driveway beside her, a car roared under the impatient foot of her brother.

We're all home, she thought wearily. All seven of us.

Phyl stood for a moment with her hand on the doorknob. She heard running footsteps, and the door opened. A second later Phyl was in the grasp of a five-year-old's bearhug.

"Pill! I missed you! Where were you? Play with me!"

Phyl allowed herself to be led into the house by Suzie. Would she ever learn to say "Phyl" instead of "Pill?" Phyl wondered. The memory of the other question faded behind the chatter of her little sister.

2
Making Money

"Remember the meeting and bring your list," Pat called to Phyl as she left the group and walked toward her house. The girls had agreed not to discuss the money-making projects until the meeting. Each was to list as many things as she could think of, and they would compare lists at the meeting. Phyl waved in agreement and disappeared into the house, the other three continuing on.

"I hope someone has had better luck than me," commented Andy. "My best plan so far is to rob a bank."

Marty made big eyes and stared at Andy. "We promised not to tell until the meeting."

"Can't you ever be serious for a minute?" Pat scolded Andy.

"What good does it do? Last night I told my mother I wanted to get paid for sitting Gwennie. She told me I already was getting paid—three meals a day."

"Sounds like my luck," said Pat. "I offered to wash my brother's car for a dollar, and he said, for that price he'd wait for rain."

Andy was silent. She waved good-bye as she turned toward her house, and Pat and Marty walked on.

"How much money are we doing to need?" Marty asked.

"I'm afraid to think about it," Pat answered as they parted.

Later, four girls and four lists clustered around the clubhouse table.

"Let's start alphabetically. Andy first," suggested Pat.

Phyl's throat tightened. Andy first—as always. Phyl forced her tongue to be silent. What did it matter who was first? They were all in it together.

30

Andy read her list. "Babysitting; lawn mowing; car washing; weed pulling. That's all I could think of," she apologized.

Marty giggled and read her list. "Babysitting; lawn mowing; car washing; weed pulling."

"Hey, you cheated," yelled Andy. "You copied my list."

"Did not," insisted Marty. "It's just that great minds think of the same things."

Pat looked around the group. "You're not going to believe my list. Babysitting." The girls smiled. "Lawn mowing." The girls giggled. "Car washing." With that, all four girls dissolved in laughter.

When it quieted down, Mary asked, "Is the other one 'weed pulling' by any chance?"

"Nope," said Pat; "gardening." Once again, the four were on the floor laughing.

When they stopped to catch their breath, Andy voiced the obvious, "That's the same thing."

"It's not spelled the same," Pat insisted.

When the laughter died down, they turned to Phyl. With great dignity, she read her list. "Lemonade stand; sewing doll clothes; paper route."

31

The three looked at each other. "Those sound good," they agreed. "What shall we try first?"

"I vote for the lemonade stand," began Andy.

"I can make the lemonade," offered Phyl. "I make it in 50-gallon vats every day for dinner. We'll need two dozen lemons, five pounds of sugar, and a sack of ice. About five dollars. We can split the cost four ways."

"We have a lot of paper cups here in the clubhouse."

"Where should we have it?"

"How about the vacant lot over on Elm Street?"

"Sounds good. When do we start? Tomorrow?"

Phyl organized them in one sentence. "I'll meet you there at nine o'clock next Saturday. Hey—that's tomorrow! You guys bring some boards and a couple of chairs to make the stand." Phyl always was good at getting the show on the road.

The meeting adjourned, but no one left quite yet. "If we sell 40 glasses at 25 cents each, that's ten dollars. Five dollars profit. That's not a bad start."

"How about 25 glasses at 40 cents a glass?"

asked Marty hopefully, but she was ignored entirely.

On Saturday morning Phyl was the first to arrive. She set the lemons, sugar, and ice on a rock and looked down the street to see Marty and Pat, each with a chair. Andy followed with two boards balanced across her shoulders.

Not bad, Phyl told herself. We'll have customers just to see what we're doing.

Phyl set the chairs back to back, about three feet apart, and slipped the boards through the backs of the chair, making two shelves. She set the mixing bowl on one of the chairs and dissolved the sugar in a small amount of water. When the sugar was a liquid, all four ground the pulp and juice from the lemons. Finally the ice went into the bowl, and the lemonade was ready to taste. Phyl poured a half-glass for each of them and waited for comments. She felt pretty good about her work. Coming from a large family, she had lots of experience doing lots of things.

"Perfect," judged Marty. "Almost as good as I could have done."

"Maybe we'll let *you* make it next time," joked Pat.

"All we need now is a customer."

"And here he comes," said Marty, her finger pointing to a little spotted dog wagging his tail and watching from a distance.

"Go away, little doggie. You're bad for business. Unless you have money, that is."

The dog sat on the ground and continued to wag his tail. The brushing of his tail stirred up a small dust cloud which drifted up in the breeze.

"Not in my lemonade you don't!" yelled Phyl, jumping toward the dog—which ran away.

The next living thing to come along was the mailman. "Any good?" he asked.

"We'll never tell," said Andy, "but you can find out for a quarter."

The mailman grinned and took the coin from his pocket. Phyl poured a glass for him.

"Hmmm—very good!" he observed as he drained the glass. "Just see that you're here every day that the temperature is above 70." The mailman picked up his bag and waved good-luck.

The next customer was not soon in coming. The girls wandered around, then finally sat on the ground. Phyl anxiously examined the ice in the drink. "If we don't sell this pretty soon, it'll be too weak."

"Maybe this wasn't such a good location," Marty decided.

A car pulled over to the curb, and the girls turned to meet the customer. Wide-eyed, Marty nudged Andy in the ribs. "First the Post Office, and now the police. The President will be by next."

The policeman walked up to the stand. "How's business?"

"If you buy something, you'll be the second," Phyl told him, handing him a glassfull.

The policeman didn't seem in a hurry. He looked over their stand and stirred the lemonade thoughtfully. The girls watched every move.

"Did you really sell some?" he asked.

"The postman bought a glass. He said it was good."

"I'm sure it is, but there's a little problem here. In this town, anyone who sells food or drink must have a food handler's permit. I don't suppose you have one? In your cash register, maybe?"

Phyl shook her head. "Marty's pocket is the cash register, and all that's in there is a quarter."

The policeman shook his head, stroked his chin and stared into the lemonade. A flying insect dipped its wings and landed in the icy drink. The policeman quickly picked out the bug and flung it to the ground.

Andy was quiet. Pat and Phyl watched the policeman carefully, but Marty asked, "Is it legal to put twelve-year-old kids in jail?"

The policeman grinned. "How much money do you have invested in this venture?"

This was Phyl's department. "Five sixty-five. Why?"

"It's just that I know a bunch of thirsty men back at headquarters who might be interested in giving you back your investment. It really is against the law to sell this, but we can help you break even. Would you like to?"

By now, any way out seemed good. "We'd love to," they agreed.

As the policeman drove away with his paid-for lemonade, the girls sat back on the ground and looked at each other. Not so good. People don't get rich by breaking even. As soon as the policeman returned with Phyl's mother's bowl, they would proceed to another item on their get-rich list.

"How about washing cars?" Marty began. "With four of us, that should be easy."

"Especially all those little foreign jobs," added Pat.

"We could divide up, two to a street, and each take one side. If we find a customer, we write down the address and say we'll be back this afternoon," decided Phyl, the organizer.

"How much do we charge?" Andy wanted to know.

"How about a buck, considering we're new at it."

"Eight cars in one day, eight bucks—that's way more than we'd make on lemonade."

When the policeman returned with the bowl, he complimented the girls. "Very good. Too bad you couldn't operate the stand."

After he left, Phyl said, "I guess we're ready. I'll take one side of Elm so I can take the bowl home, and we can meet at the clubhouse in an hour. Okay?"

"Okay," they agreed.

An hour later three girls met at the clubhouse to compare notes. They each had signed up one customer.

"Where's Andy?" Phyl asked.

"Maybe she got a lot of jobs," Pat decided. "I hope so. I had rotten luck. Everybody on my street said their dad or son was supposed to do the car today."

"Anyway, we have three. That's three dollars, even if Andy doesn't get any."

The door opened and Andrea came in silently.

"So you remembered. We thought you were going into business for yourself."

"No—everyone just wanted to tell me their life's story. I even had to look at one old lady's flowers in her back yard. And after that she didn't want her car washed." Then she added, "Um-m . . . do we want to wash a bus for two dollars?"

"A bus?"

"I told him we'd do it, but we can back out if you want to."

"Hey—that's worth two cars! Let's go and do it now."

An hour later Pat commented, "I didn't realize a bus has a million windows." She was rubbing wadded newspaper over the windows; her brothers had said it would make the glass shine. "I could have sworn this bus had only a couple hundred when I started."

"Shut up and keep thinking; two dollars, two dollars, two dollars," Marty suggested.

"I finished polishing the chrome," announced Andy as the three watched Pat scrub the corners of the last window.

"Look!" yelled Marty and pointed to the rear of the bus. A large sheet of soap suds was easing over the back of the bus and slipping down, thoroughly smearing Pat's windows and Andy's chrome.

"Didn't anyone rinse the top?" cried Phyl. They looked at each other blankly.

"Then I suppose we better do it now."

"Maybe the sun will dry it," Pat suggested hopefully. "No, I guess not. We'd better rinse it."

Phyl aimed the stream of water onto the top of the bus. Soapy water streamed down all sides while Marty and Andy cried on each other's shoulders.

"We'll all polish; it won't take so long," comforted Phyl as she distributed wads of newspaper.

When the monstrous bus was again dry and shiny, they stood back to view their handiwork.

"I wouldn't touch that thing again for less than five bucks!" Marty announced flatly. "Let's go collect."

Phyl knocked at the door. When the man opened it, she announced, "We're finished."

"Hmmm," the man said as he looked toward the bus. "I'll have to go out and look it over."

Marty nudged Andy. "For two measly dollars he has to inspect it?"

Andy sighed. "I can't possibly polish that thing again."

The man checked the wheels and chrome, the license plate the headlight. Then, as the last straw, he stepped on the bumper and looked on top.

"Pretty good; pretty good," he commented. "Figured you girls did sloppy work when you only charged two dollars. I usually pay at least five." The man took out his billfold. "Who's the treasurer of your bunch?"

The girls looked at Andy; after all, she had gotten the job for them, even if she did undercharge.

The man looked at Andy. She was a mess. Her hair was wet and stringy, and her jeans soaked and dirty. Then he took out a five-dollar bill and handed it to her. "It'll take the other three dollars to buy soap to clean you up." The man smiled as he looked around at the four smiles and four pairs of sparkling eyes. "No hugs or kisses—please! You're all too dirty." He grinned and returned to his house, leaving the four dazed girls standing speechless at the curb.

Andy was the first to get her voice. "Guess what would have happened if we had left the soap on top." The others nodded knowingly.

Washing the other three cars was like play compared to the huge bus, but there were no more tips. The day's wages totaled eight dollars and looked impressive as they spread it on the clubhouse table.

"The trouble with car washing, you can only do it once a week. We need something else."

"How about the paper route?"

"You really think we could?"

"I don't know why not. Boys do it all the time—even boys a lot younger than us."

"Yeah—but we're not boys."

"Can they kill us for trying?" asked Phyl. "It's

too late today, but now that school is out, we can go Monday."

"What else can we do? We still have a couple of hours before supper."

"Did we rule out lawn mowing?"

Andy brightened. "We have a mower in the garage, and gas too. Do you know how to start one?"

"No," said Pat, "but one of my brothers can show us. I think Jason's home now."

"Let's go."

The girls got the mower out of the garage with no trouble and pushed it toward Pat's house. "Has anyone ever mowed?" Phyl asked. "We don't even know how."

"What's to know? You just push it along and follow it. My brothers do it all the time."

When they got to Pat's house, Jason insisted on knowing the whole story before helping them. "I ought to tell Mom. She wouldn't let you do this, you know. You kids are pretty little yet."

"Well, we were big enough to earn eight dollars washing cars today, so we're big enough to mow lawns, too. Besides, with four of us, we won't get tired," Pat assured him.

42

Jason still looked doubtful. He turned the switch and gave the rope a sharp yank. The motor popped a couple of times and then settled down to an ear-splitting roar. He turned it off and told Pat, "Now you try it."

Pat turned the switch and pulled the rope. Nothing.

"Let me," requested Phyl, but her attempt was no better.

"Both of you try it together," suggested Jason—and this time the motor caught.

"How much gas do you have," he asked as he opened the gas tank and looked in. "You don't have enough to mow 20 feet." He took a can from the ground beside his car and poured gas into the mower. "Now if your business folds, it isn't my fault."

"How much should we charge?"

"Depends on the size of the yard. Anywhere from five to ten dollars—fifteen if it's huge. But you better stick to small ones."

They thanked him and turned to leave, but he caught Pat by the shoulder. "If you tell Mom I helped you, I'll choke you," Jason threatened.

"Who? Me? What help?" Pat teased.

43

Two blocks away they finally found a yard with grass high enough for cutting.

"How much for this one," Marty asked.

"It's too big for a five-dollar yard. How about seven-fifty?"

"Maybe seven."

"Sounds about right."

Marty walked alone up to the door and knocked. When the man answered, the others could see she was having a little trouble convincing him. He kept looking at the three girls waiting on the sidewalk. Marty held up four fingers and shook her head. The man went back into the house, and Marty joined the others.

"We can do it for seven, but he hopes there's only four of us. I told him that was all. Let's get started."

"This thing is going to take two of us to push," said Andy. "Who's going to help me?"

Marty joined Andy at the handle. "Will I do?"

"Sure," said Phyl, "but we'll start it. Jason showed us how," she bragged. "Come on, Pat." Two tugs and the machine burped into action.

Andy and Marty guided the mower into line with the fence and pushed. By the time they had made one circle, they were able to guide it evenly and were ready to make the next turn.

At that moment a shiny black car stopped at the curb and Andy's face turned pale.

While the four girls watched, the car door opened and Andrea's mother stepped out. "I thought that looked like you pushing the lawnmower. Whatever are you doing? Don't you know that a lawnmower is very dangerous and you might get hurt?"

Andy hung her head and said nothing.

"I think you should get into the car; we'll talk about it," her mother continued.

Andy looked at the other girls.

"That's all right," they said. "We'll finish."

Andy followed her mother to the car.

"Andrea," her mother began as they drove away, "I'm sorry to have to bring you home, but you must understand how I feel. You are the only child God has given me. Perhaps mothers with several children do not feel this way, but I'm so afraid you will be hurt. You do understand, don't you?"

Andy nodded. Yes, after all these years, she did understand.

"Why were you mowing the yard there, anyway?"

Andy hesitated, but decided she would have to explain. "Mother, it was for the club. We wanted to earn some money so we could buy a cassette recorder. We need to tape our singing and see for ourselves how we sound."

"But Andrea, you know I would have bought one for you if you had only asked."

"I know, Mother; but it isn't the same. It would be mine. This will be ours."

"Yes, I see. But before you do anything else, please talk with me. I just might understand." Andy's mother smiled at her, and Andy returned the smile. When they reached their house, Andy excused herself and went to the clubhouse.

When the door was safely locked behind her, she sat down at the table and buried her face in her arms. Her sobs shook the table, and tears soaked her arm. If the clubhouse had ears, it would have heard this many times before.

Later, when the others girls appeared at the clubhouse, Andy was dry-eyed and smiling again.

"My mother was only worried about me. You know how she is. But, guess what! She did say I

46

could help with the paper route if we go in pairs. You know—two in the morning and two in the evening."

Marty had stretched out on the floor, and Pat and Phyl were slumped in chairs. "I wish my mother had come by and taken me home. I've never been so tired in all my life. How do boys push one of those things all alone over a whole yard?"

Pat and Phyl shook their heads in wondering agreement.

"Delivering papers has to be easier," they agreed.

On Monday they biked to the office of the newspaper route manager and asked for the job. The expresson on his face was so incredible that they would have laughed if they had dared.

"But, I've never hired girls before. Besides, I don't have four routes available."

"Oh, we don't want four; just one that we can share."

The manager bowed his head and rubbed his eyes—as if he thought this might be a dream and

47

would go away. He opened his eyes . . . and the four girls were still waiting for an answer.

"Now, let me get this straight. All four of you girls want to work on one route?"

The girls nodded. "Two of us in the morning, and two in the afternoon," Phyl explained.

"If I hire you, you have to work for 30 days, whether you like it or not. And you have to tell me two weeks before you quit so that I can hire someone else."

Their eyes brightened when it sounded as if they would get the job.

The manager looked at each girl carefully and then spoke to Phyl. "Write down all four names," he told her, "and come with me. I'll explain what you do."

He told them they would have to go to a drop-off station to get the papers. Then they had to fold them. And, whether they threw the papers or carried them to the houses, the papers had to end up six feet or less from the customers' front doors. Then the manager gave them two lists. "Here are the morning customers, and these are the evening . . . and make sure they don't get mixed!"

As the girls turned to go, he began to rub his eyes again.

On the sidewalk outside, the girls screemed with laughter. "Did you hear what he said?" asked Andy. " 'What in the world have I just done?' "

"And did you see his face?" howled Marty.

Most of all, though, their laughter came from happiness. They really had a paper route, and it was going to be fun.

"Let's ride the route now so we learn it," Phyl suggested. "And we have to decide who takes what route. I want afternoons because my mother needs me at breakfast."

"I have to take mornings because of piano practice," reasoned Andy.

"I can't wake up in the morning, so I'll go with Phyl," decided Marty.

They all three looked at Pat. "Now, which one should I take," she clowned. "I believe I would really like to take the morning. Especially since that's all that's left."

Pat turned to Andy. "Let's look at the route carefully. Next time we see it, the sun won't be up yet."

The paper route worked well. When it came time to collect, Phyl and Marty, the evening deliverers, stopped at their customers' houses and were invited in. They were given lemonade and tips. It was a novelty to have a girl paper boy, and those customers who had watched for their papers had seen the girls riding by on their bicycles each evening.

Pat and Andy had a harder time collecting. Most of their customers hadn't been awake to see the delivery. So, at collection time, they almost refused to believe the two little girls were their paper "boys." Three times Pat had to offer to call the company to prove it.

"It's not fair," decided Pat and Andy when they saw that the other pair received more in tips than they had.

However, when they sorted the bills and stacked the coins, all four girls were impressed. The recorder seemed like a reality for the first time. They decided to give up car washing and lawn mowing entirely.

"I sure am glad of that," declared Marty. "That's not my kind of work."

"Me, too," agreed Andy. "Besides, I have a recital in six weeks. If I practice four hours a day between now and then, I might be ready."

"Really? Four hours? Are you kidding?"

"Don't I wish! The piece is 20 pages long, and I've never heard it before."

"Why can't you play one you already know?" Phyl asked.

"Because if I do good on a new one, I'll advance to a special teacher."

"Hey, that's great! Aren't you excited?"

"I guess. Anyway, that's what my mother wants."

After a thoughtful silence in the clubhouse, Phyl spoke. "I sure wish my mother wanted that."

There was another long pause. Then Pat said, "I vote we go to the park and feed the ducks."

"Good idea," agreed the relieved Andy. "I'll get some bread from the kitchen and meet you guys out front."

3
"Love Is Patient . . ."

The four summer-tanned girls grouped around the clubhouse table. "Just look at that pile of money," demanded the amazed Pat as the piles of coins were sorted, counted, and stacked next to the dollar bills. "I didn't realize paper boys make so much!"

"Did we keep track of how much was for papers and how much for tips?" asked Andy.

"I don't think so," answered Phyl.

"I'm glad we didn't," Andy replied. "Some people still don't believe Marty and I are bringing their papers. They hardly want to pay us. Knowing how much they got in tips would make us feel bad; huh, Marty?"

"Oh, I don't think so. I think maybe their tips would be more if they wore hose and lipstick."

"You're just jealous, Marty," accused Pat. "Besides, we've almost got enough money now."

"How much is it?"

Phyl straightened the stacks of quarters. "Sixty-seven dollars and twenty-five cents. And this week's collections haven't even been made."

"Let's go see how much recorders are," suggested Andy. "Maybe we can get it now."

Marty brightened. "Yeah, let's go now."

"Is anyone expected home for a couple hours?" asked Phyl, the unofficial chairman of the group. A chorus of no's was the answer.

"Let's go to Brown's Music Company first. That's close enough to walk."

"I wonder if we'll have a choice of color," Marty asked as they walked.

"We ought to make it match the clubhouse if we can."

"I don't think we ever decided what color the clubhouse would be."

"I voted for green a month ago, remember?" reminded Phyl.

There was a long pause for half a block.

"Hey, I have an idea," exclaimed Pat. "Let's make the clubhouse psychedelic! You know—lot's of colors!"

"Yeah, I vote for that," chimed in Marty.

"Let's pick out the recorder first," suggested Phyl.

The four walked on in silence till they reached the store entrance.

"Who's going to do the talking?" asked Phyl.

"How about you? Is that okay with the rest of you?" asked Pat.

"Fine," they agreed.

There was a light-green recorder for only $38.99; but when they played a test tape, it sounded tinny. And on medium volume the plastic rattled.

"Well," said the salesman, "if you want quality, I have some that cost a bit more."

"How much more?" asked Phyl.

"This one is $99.95. It's an AM/FM stereo recorder with two built-in condenser mikes and a five-band graphic equalizer. Runs on AC and batteries. And you won't find better speakers on a portable at twice the price." The salesman slipped in the demo tape and moved the knobs to demonstrate.

"Fantastic!" exclaimed Marty. "I vote for this one."

"But we couldn't get that till Saturday, and we can get the cheaper one now," pointed out Pat.

"But this is so much better. Let's wait."

The salesman waited patiently as an impromptu meeting was held. The girls decided to wait.

"Shall I hold it for you? If you have a small deposit, I'll fix it up for you right now."

The girls looked at each other in surprise. No one had thought of bringing money.

"How much do we have all together?" Phyl asked. Small change from leftover allowances began appearing from purses. They emptied handfuls of change on the sales counter.

"Dollar twenty-three," he told them.

"Is that enough?"

"What name shall I use?"

"All four of us. That's Andy, that's Pat, that's Phyl, and I'm Marty."

The salesman rolled his eyes and groaned, but he wrote down all four names. He was still shaking his head as the girls called, "See you Saturday," and left.

"I have an idea," announced Marty. "While we're here, let's look at sheet music. If we're going to be rich, we can buy a lot."

"Yeah; if we keep the paper route till school starts, we'll have all kinds of money in our account. How about it?"

"Okay; let's go look at the music. I'm getting bored with our same ol' songs anyway."

With that, the girls turned on their heels and went back into the store. The salesman's eyes got large and worried, but he relaxed when they passed his department in favor of records and music.

"Look! A new shipment! Lot's of new quartets."

"Hey, here's one Pastor would like. Let's remember to get it."

"Look at this one," said Phyl; "the new arrangement of *God, the Creator*."

"Really?" responded the excited girls, and

gathered around her. "But look," pointed out Marty; "that's a trio arrangement."

The girls looked at each other with long faces. "Maybe Andy would put in another part."

"Thanks," Andy said, "but I'm really not that good. Maybe we can find it in the quartet section."

Ten minutes of looking proved they could not.

When they finally gave up, Pat the peace-maker pointed out, "Oh, well, there are more pretty ones here than Andy would learn anyway with that concert she's giving."

"It's a recital," corrected Andy.

"It's all the same thing."

"No; you have to be really good to give a concert, but anybody can give a recital," Andy insisted.

"Andy, you be careful about getting any better," Marty suggested. "Before we know it, you'll refuse to play for us."

"Yes," Pat cautioned, "you mustn't forget us. We're the ones who helped you and gave you your boost to fame."

"*You* helped?" Andy wanted to know. "What did you do?"

Pat pretended to look hurt. "Have you really

forgotten all the time off we gave you from club meetings and other important gatherings?" Pat shoot her head in mock disbelief. "Could you really have forgotten to whom you owe your success? Our only requirement has been that you learn our music first, and then the rest of your practice time was on your own. For lessons and things."

Everyone laughed but Phyl. "Yeah, don't ever forget that," she added sarcastically. The laughter died quickly, and the girls walked out in silence.

When they reached Phyl's house, she turned toward the gate, "Guess I'd better check in. My mom probably has a to-do list for me a mile long."

When Phyl was out of hearing range, Marty thought out loud, "Wonder what's eating her?"

Pat, wanting to change the subject, asked Andy, "Do you have a new dress for your recital?"

"Yes. My mother picked it out and brought it home for my approval. It's okay. I don't really care."

"Can we see it?"

"Sure, come on home with me."

In Andy's room the girls gathered at the closed door.

"Oh, it's beautiful!" exclaimed Pat.

"Do you really think so?"

"I think it's gorgeous," agreed Marty. "You'll have to have your picture taken in it, sitting at the piano, looking over your shoulder." Marty demonstrated the pose—with an exaggerated smile.

"You must have read my mother's mind," Andy told them. "That's exactly what she wants. Would you like to pose for it? You seem to know a lot more about it than I do."

"Any time, friend," clowned Marty as she returned the dress to its hanger.

Phyl knew there was nothing special to be done at her house today; she just wanted to get away by herself. But that was hard to do at her house; people and activity seemed to be everywhere. Her older twin brother and sister's birthday was coming, and her sister's girl friends were helping make a huge cake. The brother just older than Phyl was mowing the lawn with his noisy, beat-up mower. Anything left on the lawn was doomed, because he invariably pulverized everything in his path. The twins just younger were playing "elevator" from the lawn to their upstairs window, hoisting toys up and down. The littlest

60

sister, Suzie, who had picked Phyl as her favorite, ran to Phyl the instant she saw her.

"Play with me," she demanded as she tried to pull Phyl by the arm.

"I don't feel like playing your game," Phyl said.

"Then I'll help you play yours," Suzie offered, not loosening her grip on Phyl's arm. "Where are you going to play?"

Phyl knew it was useless to try to get rid of her. But, then, Suzie isn't much trouble, Phyl told herself; and sometimes she even helps me get out of a blue mood.

"Let's try the yard," Phyl told her.

"Okay," the little girl agreed enthusiastically. "I'll get my new Kindergarten mat for us to sit on." In a moment she was back. "Why do they call it a Kindergarten mat when I'm going into the first grade?" Suzie had turned six earlier in the summer.

"I don't know. Maybe they thought you wouldn't be promoted. They thought you might flunk sandbox."

"Pill! Don't tease! I played gooder in sandbox than anybody!"

Phyl spread the mat among the shrubbery, clearly the most private spot available.

"Pill?"

"Yes?"

"How do we play this game?"

Phyl thought fast. "Well, you have to be very quiet and think about something a while. Then you have to tell me what you're thinking about."

The six-year-old cupped her hands under her chin and stared at her brother, mowing noisy circles in the yard. "I'm done," she announced after a minute and a half. "Do I tell it now?"

Phyl nodded.

"Well, if I was a grass, I'd be tired . . . and sad, too."

"Why?"

"Because in winter the snow buries it, and in the summer they get cut off. And in between they get walked on. But they still have to grow and stay green."

Phyl nodded. Her sister had a clear head, and this was a very good point. "Do you want to hear my thought now? It's sort of like yours."

"Did you think about grass, too?"

"No," answered Phyl. "I thought about

62

thoughts. Sometimes they get chopped off and thrown away, too—but they still grow back."

"How can you throw away a thought?"

"Well," Phyl answered, "maybe it was a bad thought and you shouldn't have it. Like a weed, you want it to go away and not ever come back—but it always does."

"Daddy says you have to dig up weeds by the root and burn 'em. Then they won't come back. Do thoughts have roots?"

"Maybe," Phyl admitted. "But I don't know how to dig them up."

"I don't know either," Suzie said thoughtfully. "I know who does, though."

"Who?"

"God. 'Cause He made us. He can get inside us and do anything He wants to. Pill, what would that feel like?"

Phyl thought a moment. "It would have to feel good," she decided.

Little Suzie bounded up from the mat and ran into the yard. "I'm going to gather enough grass to buld a bunny nest," she called to Phyl as she started to gather fresh grass clippings.

Phyl stretched out on the mat and looked at the sky. Thoughts really can be a problem, she admitted to herself. It wasn't that she didn't like Andy; they had been friends for more than six years. It just seemed that everything Andy wanted, she got. It was like their prayers got mixed up. Phyl got the people, and Andy got the things. Phyl would never want another thing in the world if she only had a piano. Andy got tired of practicing, but Phyl could think of nothing more wonderful than to sit at that big, beautiful piano and make it sound like Andy did.

It wasn't so bad at first when there were lots of games to play with Pat and Marty while Andy played one-finger pieces. Sometimes Phyl even felt sorry for Andy because she couldn't play games with them all the time. Now it seemed like everyone at church and school and everywhere thought Andy was just grand because of what she could do.

If I had gotten a chance like that, I could have done even better than Andy, Phyl told herself.

Phyl could feel the jealousy growing. She was not fooled; she knew it for what it was. Sometimes her tongue hurt from biting it to keep from saying something hateful. But she couldn't always stop it. "Out of the overflow of the heart the mouth speaks." She had learned in Sunday school that Jesus had said that. Right, she admitted to herself. My mouth is the weed and my heart the root.

No matter how many times she cut off the weed, the jealousy was back.

Help me, help me, help me! The words ran through her mind pleadingly. Dear Jesus, I know You know what's best for me, but I just don't understand why I can't have this one thing. You know I would use a piano for Your glory. Why? Why?"

From the yard a voice called, "Look, Pill; I made a green mountain. Watch me move it with one kick." With that, Suzie ran through the pile. The fresh grass flew into the air and covered her hair and clothing.

Phyl's mind drifted back to her problem. Funny thing about those Bible verses teachers made you learn, ones that didn't seem to mean anything. They suddenly popped back in your mind just when you felt like you didn't need them. Phyl had an immediate problem with one from

1 Corinthians 13: "If I . . . have not love, I am nothing. . . . Love is patient, love is kind." But how long do you have to be patient?

Phyl did love Andy, and she was kind to her most of the time. Phyl just had more pain than she was able to take. Yet, "[God] will not let you be tempted beyond what you can bear. But when you are tempted, he will also provide a way out."

*Where, Lord? I live here, and I see Andy and her piano every day. Where is **my** way out?*

Her thoughts were interrupted by her sister again. "I want a bath and start all over; I itch." Phyl watched Suzie's flying heels dash toward the house.

I itch too, Phyl thought, *but I can't seem to start all over. There's too much to forget.*

She tried to pry the problem from her mind. If she tried very hard, she'd conquer these thoughts, Phyl promised herself, forgetting the passage where Jesus had said: "What is impossible with men is possible with God."

Phyl focused her attention on the new song with the trio arrangement. Why shouldn't they use it? It wouldn't be like anyone was left out. Andy played the piano, so she would still be part of the group. Why should she get to sing and play both—all of the time? Really, she shouldn't mind.

Oh, no! There it was again. Phyl had just chopped off the jealousy weed, yet there it was again—big and green. Phyl was suddenly very lonesome for the other girls. Maybe they were at the clubhouse.

She got up quickly and walked around the house to the front gate so her little sister wouldn't see her leave.

The clubhouse door was open and Phyl entered. Pat and Marty were lying on the floor with their legs perpendicular up the wall, their newest form of excercise. Phyl scanned the room for the fourth member. Then she remembered, this was practice time. Andy was a creature of habit and routine. Nothing, but nothing, interferred with practice time. You could set a clock by it.

"What's new?" Phyl asked.

"Andy's dress, for one thing," Marty informed her. "The one for the concert—I mean, the recital. It's beautiful!"

"I'll bet it is. All it takes is money." Phyl's

heart sank as the words were uttered. Where did those terrible things come from? "I mean, it's nice to have money to do things like that," she corrected hastily.

Pat and Marty were silent.

Phyl tried another line of conversation. "Do you think Andy would mind if we got the trio arrangement just this once? She'll be playing it anyway, you know. Maybe we could ask her."

It was a long minute before Pat answered. "Even if she did mind, she wouldn't say so."

Marty agreed. "We've always been a quartet. Maybe they could order us a special arrangement. We could ask."

Phyl nodded and said nothing more.

Marty turned to Pat. "Isn't our time up yet? How long will we have to do this before we're beautiful?"

"For you, a long time," Pat joked. Then, looking at her watch, she said to Phyl and Marty, "Hey, you two are late for the paper route. You want to get us fired?"

Two pairs of legs hit the floor, and Marty flew toward the door, grabbing Phyl's arm as she went.

The meeting of the Us 4 Ever Club was adjourned for the moment.

4
Quartet or Trio?

"Just look at that beautiful thing! And we earned every penny for it!" exclaimed Marty as she backed off to admire the new recorder, gracing their clubhouse table.

Pat looked squarely at Marty. "Just how *do* you earn a tip?"

"I'll never tell," Marty retorted. "Wild horses couldn't drag it out of me."

Phyl was thumbing through the instruction book. "Here we are. 'Rules of Operation. One: Depress Power button.'"

"Sounds logical," agreed Marty.

"To record, simultaneously depress Play and Record," she continued, and Marty complied; "and your unit is ready to record. When finished, press Stop. To play back, depress Rewind. Rewind will automatically stop at the beginning of the tape. Then depress Play."

Marty depressed and re-depressed as told.

Phyl's voice came from the recorder and told them, " . . . and your unit is ready to record. When finished, press Stop. To play back, depresses Rewind. Rewind . . . " Click—Marty turned it off.

The girls laughed with excited pleasure. "Didn't anyone ever tell you to finish your sentences?" Marty scolded the recorder.

"Boy, are we going to have fun with this thing!" decided Pat.

Andy, who had been sitting at the table with her chin in her hands admiring the new appliance, suddenly jumped to her feet. "Time to practice. I sure don't want to, but I have to."

"Can't you skip just one day? This is a special occasion."

Andy shook her head sadly and left the clubhouse.

"I have an idea," Pat said. "Let's record her recital piece."

Marty grabbed the recorder, and the three caught up with Andy in her room.

"Wait till we're ready," Marty told Andy, her fingers poised over the keys. "Now!" Marty said as she depressed Play and Record.

Andy struck the first notes just a bit hesitantly, then began to play the runs with confidence. She moved smoothly into the part when the bells tinkled lightly, and then started with the drum sounds. It was hard to make a piano sound like an entire band. The bells weren't very hard, and the drums were easy; but the wind instruments had given her a lot of trouble. Andy held her breath through the trumpet solo and breathed only lightly as her right hand became a piccolo.

Marty held her finger to her lips and looked at the others. Andy had never done so well.

Then Andy was back on the drums, and all four girls breathed again. They remembered that another hard part would come on the bottom half of the fifth page. Their muscles were tense. They had heard her play this often enough to know when she did well, and this time she was almost perfect.

Here it was—the drum beat was picked up by the trumpet and handed back to the piccolo. Not a single mistake. Beautiful! No one breathed as Andy's left hand joined her right and the piccolo duet faded into the woods in a series of echoes.

Phyl, stretched out on the carpet, had let her mind pick up the haunting sounds. It was beautiful—truly so! She could lose herself completely in music like that; she could listen to it the rest of her life.

Then the room was quiet, and Phyl heard the click of the Stop button as Marty turned off the recorder.

"It must be the recorder," Andy answered their unspoken question. "I've never played this without a mistake before."

"I have an idea," smiled Pat. "When you give the recital, we'll play the tape, and you fake it with your fingers. Perfection! Right?"

Andy nodded. "Don't I wish! The recital is only three weeks away. Even though I've spent over a hundred hours on that piece, I still have almost that many more to go."

"But just think what it sounds like," Phyl added, remembering the piccolos' fading tones. The other girls were silent, hesitating to break into Phyl's mood. "Let's not erase that tape," Phyl added. "Then we can listen to it again and again."

"I think Phyl should have that tape," decided Andy. "She's the one who likes music."

Phyl sat up suddenly. "But I don't have any way of playing it."

"Leave it at the clubhouse with the recorder."

Phyl looked at Pat and Marty. "I really would like to have it . . . if the rest of you don't mind."

"We can always make another one if we need it," pointed out Pat. "Right now, let's take this thing back to the clubhouse so Andy can practice."

The recorder took a place of honor on the clubhouse table. Phyl rewound the tape, set the volume, and cradled her head in her arms on the table. Her mind turned off the rest of the world as she settled down to enjoy the music.

Pat and Marty began examining the walls and furniture. Phyl heard nothing as they discussed re-covering the sofa and chair, donated six years before by Andy's parents.

"I think purple velvet would be nice," decided Pat.

"Let's ask Phyl what she thinks," suggested Marty. But when they turned to Phyl and saw the closed eyes and dreamy expression, they decided to wait.

Sometime later, as the drums handed the beat to the trumpets, and they changed it from a staccato to a melody and passed it to the piccolo, Phyl raised her head and rubbed her eyes. Back to reality again. It was only a dream . . . and the music was not hers, only a cassette.

Pat brought up the question. "What do you think of purple velvet slipcovers?"

Phyl thought about it, still half-listening to the music in the background. "Maybe we ought to wait for Andy; it's her clubhouse."

Marty looked at Pat. Pat's lips tightened as she looked at the floor. "Sure, but we're just talking now. The clubhouse really belongs to all of us. That's what her dad said. He said we could come here anytime we wanted."

The music stopped and Phyl pressed a button on the recorder. "You know what I mean," Phyl replied. "It's her yard, her piano, her music. And we have to adjust everything to her schedule. Are you forgetting all the times we waited for her to finish practicing, or went on without her? Really, we're a trio more than a quartet. I think we should get that trio arrangement and anything else we want. With all she has, she'll never care."

Pat and Marty were silent. Pat was the first to break the stillness. "I think we should plan a picnic or outing before school starts again. What do you think, Marty?"

Marty looked at her in amazement. "You're reading my mind! I was just going to tell you. My parents are going camping in a couple of weeks, and they said I could invite you guys."

"Hey, yeah!" they agreed. "Where are you going?"

"Probably Lake Catherine."

"Isn't that close to Eagle's Nest Peak?"

"I think so."

"Then let's climb it," suggested Phyl. "I've always wanted to go have a picnic lunch up there."

"That'd be fun," Marty agreed. "How about you, Pat?"

"Do you think we can do it? That trail is so

hard that my brothers had to climb it for a Boy Scout endurance test."

"Sure," said Phyl. "The Us 4 Ever Club is as good as any bunch of boys. At least if we take it slow."

"Maybe we could, but what about Andy? She gets tired so easy. You know how she is."

Phyl's jealousy got the better of her. "Yes, I know how she is. It's always 'Andy, Andy, Andy.' Why is it always Andy who shapes our plans? We manage alright when she's practicing that piano. Why not now? Why don't we do what *we* want, not just what suits Andy?"

Silence.

"Well, I think it'd be lot's of fun, myself," Marty said. "Andy could even go along. If we take it real slow and remember to help her, she might not have any trouble. Anyhow, let's talk more about it later. We have a date with the newspaper office. We've got a remodeling job to pay for."

Marty left, with Phyl following. Pat decided to go home rather than wait for Andy, so she closed the clubhouse door.

Andy was just finishing her piece the last time

for the day as her mother's car pulled into the driveway. Andy's heart thumped a little harder. Maybe her mother wouldn't have a meeting or anything tonight and they could have supper together and just talk. Andy had a lot to say. Her mother would be pleased that the girls liked the dress she had picked out, and that Andy had played the recital piece without a mistake. She could even prove it with the tape ... if her mother was that interested.

Andy jumped up from the piano and ran down the stairs. She had to hurry before her mother came in the door, or her mother would scold her for running. It was hard being an only child. Andy's mother wouldn't let her do anything she thought was dangerous. After all, Andy asked herself, how many twelve-year-olds fall on a stairway?

"Hello, Sweetheart," her mother greeted. "Had a nice day?"

"Oh, yes, Mother. We got the recorder." Andy knew she should talk slower so the conversation would last longer; that way, her mother might not leave the house so soon. But Andy was so excited she couldn't wait. "I played the new piece, and we recorded it. And, guess what. I didn't make even one tiny little mistake."

"Why, that's wonderful, Darling! All your hard work is beginning to pay off. Did you keep the tape?"

"I gave it to Phyl, but it's still in the club-house—if you want to hear it."

"Sometime," her mother promised.

"Mother, have you noticed how much some people like music? I mean, more than other people."

"Why, yes, Dear. You enjoy your music, don't you?"

"Sure, but not near as much as Phyl does. When I was playing for the recorder, she lay on the floor with her eyes closed—like she was in another world."

Her mother turned toward her. "Really? I must hear that tape sometime."

Andy kept talking. "If Phyl had a piano and lessons, she would be really, really good. I think she'd be a lot better than I ever will."

Andy heard her mother sigh softly. "Andrea, not everyone has a chance to have everything they want. We have to make the best of what we have.

Doesn't Phyl's daddy work in town here and come home every night? Doesn't Phyl have brothers and sisters in her family? Remember how excited you were when her new sister was born, and you wanted one just like her?"

Andy and her mother looked at each other for a long moment.

"I know, Mother. That's how I know Phyl wants a piano. It's a want that won't die." Andy followed along to her mother's room. "Will you be staying home this evening?"

"I wish I could, Darling; but we're having a flower show at the church tomorrow, and I have to make a lot of arrangements. I'm truly sorry. Perhaps the girls could come over and stay a while. You could make candy or cookies. How does that sound?"

"All right; I'll see if they can come." And, for a minute or two, Andy really thought she would call the others. But some lonesome feelings even a friend can't help.

Andy went to her room and sat at the piano. Maybe being able to play the piano wasn't exactly all she wanted, but it was always there—and no one could take it away from her. She struck at the keys, playing the hard part of her recital piece—the wind instruments—and tried to picture each one in her mind, as her teacher had instructed.

Momentarily, she looked toward the window and saw a light in the clubhouse. If someone wasn't there, she should make sure the light was turned off. Hearing her mother's car leave the driveway, Andy ran down the stairs.

Inside the clubhouse, she looked around. Empty. The others had just forgotten to turn out the light.

As Andy started across the room, she saw the soft red glow of the recorder's light. They had left that on, too. She punched the rewind button. What was there about that music that made Phyl so quiet and dreamy? Maybe if Andy played it now, it would help her understand. Anyway, there was nothing else to do. There was no one at home, so she might just as well be alone here in the clubhouse.

Andy cringed as the first hesitant notes were struck. Why couldn't she remember to begin loud and strong as her teacher kept telling her? By the fifth measure, she was better. Andy listened critically to the sound of her own fingers. "This really isn't bad at all," she said to no one.

The recording was coming to the hard part. Unconsciously, Andy held her breath. There was the pause . . . and then the soft little sounds of the clarinet materialized from nowhere.

Andy began to feel strange and light-headed, like she was the only person in the woods, and all the instruments were speaking to her. Was this they way Phyl felt? Andy stretched out on the floor, imitating Phyl, hoping to capture her ecstacy.

The sound filled the room and pressed in on her. Andy closed her eyes and went back to the woods. Here came the drums, faintly at first, then louder and louder. The trumpets joined in and changed the beat to a melody. They lifted it higher and higher, and Andy could see the piccolo become two piccolos, walking off together. She knew they would be leaving, but her mind tried to hold them for another second or two. They wouldn't stay. Now they were gone, and there was an echo . . . then a fainter echo . . . and then silence.

Andy couldn't move. Did Phyl feel this way? The mood of the music had held her tightly to the floor. Now it was over.

"You know what I mean," the recorder continued after a click. "Look around. It's her yard, her piano, her music. And we have to adjust everything to her schedule. Are you forgetting all the . . ."

Instantly Andy realized what had happened. Phyl's afternoon conversation was being played back for her.

"With all she has, she'll never care."

"With all I have," Andy said back. "Don't they know that all I have is them?"

Andy knew she should turn off the sound, but she couldn't move. She heard Marty tell about the camping trip, and Phyl suggest Eagle's Nest. She heard Pat point out Andy's own disabilities—which were very real; for years Andy couldn't keep up.

Then Andy heard the crushing blow delivered by Phyl. "Yes, I know how she is. It's always 'Andy, Andy, Andy.' Why is it always Andy who shapes our plans? We manage alright when she's practicing that piano. Why not now? Why don't we do what *we* want, not just what suits Andy?"

Andrea leaned over to the recorder and pushed Stop, then Rewind. She found the end of her music, the exit of the piccolos and the double echo, and then pushed the Erase button. No one else should ever hear those painful words—or know that she had heard them. Things were bad enough the way it was.

Plans must be made, Andy told herself. There must be some reason I can't go on the hike. It must be normal-sounding. Wait! Pat said the hike was dangerous. Mother has a reputation for being overly protective. Why not use that? I wouldn't be lying. I'll just let the girls assume that's the reason.

Andy sat down by the recorder and buried her face in her arms. Her eyes filled with tears, but she was too weary to cry. Finally she dropped off in an exhausted sleep.

Hours later, she startled awake. It must be terribly late, she thought. Mother should be home by now and is probably worried.

Andy tiptoed into the house and up the stairs to her room. Apparently, her mother hadn't looked into Andy's room when she came home.

Andy's alarm clock buzzed her into conscious-ness, and she remembered the paper route.

Quickly she dressed and met Pat at the clubhouse. As they walked together to get their bicycles, Pat told of the camping invitation.

"We'll have a ball—staying overnight and everything! Phyl suggested we might hike to Eagle's Nest Peak."

Yes, Andy remembered. Who could forget it? Smile, Andrea; don't let them know. Keep it up. Pretend.

She put a false eagerness into her voice. "That sounds like lots of fun. I'll have to ask my mom, of course."

"Do you think she'll let you?"

"I don't know," was the honest answer. "You know how she's always afraid I'm going to get hurt."

The girls got their papers from the drop-off point and started their delivery. They had learned to hit the doorsteps now, and sometimes they even enjoyed the job . . . unless it rained.

That afternoon, the Us 4 Ever Club met in the clubhouse. Andy had just used her kitchen to make an enormous batch of oatmeal cookies to replenish the clubhouse cookie jar, and the girls were now sampling her product.

"Andy, you didn't tell us yet if you can go on the trip," Marty pointed out.

After a moment's silence, Andy said softly, "I'm sorry, but you know how things are at my house."

Good work, Andy told herself. You said nothing about your mother, so it can't be a lie.

"You guys have a lot of fun. I can use the time practicing. I'll be thinking about you."

The other three stared at her dumbly. How could she be so calm? Their most important outing of the year, and she sat there quietly and said she couldn't go. It gave them a shaky feeling—like sitting on a chair with three legs.

"Maybe if we talked with your mother and told her we would look out for you, she would change her mind," Marty reasoned. "My mother will be there; she'd be glad to watch out for you."

Andy's eyes showed just a shadow of fright. "Oh, please, no. I really need the practice time, anyway." Then she changed the subject so she wouldn't cry. "Have we decided on a color for this dump yet? I think purple velvet would be nice for the slipcovers."

The other girls were relieved as the strain of the crisis passed.

"Yeah, and maybe the walls could have swirls and flowers and lots of wild colors," Phyl decided. "We have enough money right now to buy the stuff."

"Let's go shopping tomorrow. What do we need besides paint and slipcovers?"

"Maybe some wild posters."

The next day, as the department store opened, four impatient girls almost ran to the counter bulging with drapery materials. The beautiful brocades and satins hardly got a glance as they looked for the purple velvet. When they found it, they agreed—that's exactly what they wanted. No mistake.

Marty's mother had given them instructions on how much to buy. As the shimmering folds were being measured by the clerk, Phyl wandered off by herself. When the velvet was measured, the others began to look for her. They soon spied her, motioning them to hurry over to where she was.

Stretched up a wall before her was a set of patterns and suggested colors for decorating game room walls. Flowers, swirls, blocks, designs of every kind! Just trace them on the wall, outline in black, and paint in any flashy color desired.

Without discussion the girls made a unanimous decision. This they had to have. It would require a lot of money and take days to do, but this was it.

Andy pointed out to herself, this will give me something to do while the others are on the hike.

"It's going to take two trips to get everything home, anyway," Marty noted, "so let's not buy the paint now; just the velvet and patterns. Then we can have a meeting to decide what colors we want inside the designs."

Later that day, as three girls prepared to return to the store while Andy practiced, Marty announced seriously, "This is a club meeting, whether you know it or not. Something terrible has happened. My mom called Andy's mom to tell her Andy would be safe if she went on that campout with us."

"What did Andy's mom say?"

Marty's face had a strange look as she explained, "She didn't know anything about the trip, and she hadn't told Andy she couldn't go. In fact, she told my mom she thought the camp-out would be good for Andy, and that Andy *could* go, as long as someone stayed with her all the time. And she said she appreciated the club since it meant so much to Andy."

"That's weird!" Phyl said.

"There must be a reason Andy doesn't want to go," added Pat. "She always agrees with the club's decisions. This isn't like her at all."

They puzzled over the situation all the way to and from the store. Their final decision was to ask Andy herself.

When Andy's practice time was over and she met the others in the clubhouse, Marty faced her with the dilemma. "Why don't you want to go with us? We know it isn't your mother, because she didn't even know about the trip. But she knows now, and she doesn't care if you go. So, why don't you want to?"

Andy hung her head, and an ear-splitting silence filled the room.

Finally she said, "It isn't that I don't want to

go. I always want to go. It's just . . . I'm always such a drag. Either my mother won't let me go, or I can't do stuff as well as you guys. Someone's always helping me. If I went on that hike, you couldn't go as far or do as much as you want. You'll have more fun without me."

Pat looked Andy squarely in the face. "Hear this! If you don't go, no one is going. And if I don't go, I will be very angry at whoever kept me from going. Do you understand?"

Andy broke into a slight smile, and she looked at the others gratefully.

Phyl saw the look of relief on Andy's face. Phyl hadn't realized how hard it must be to always be behind, not to be able to quite keep up, not to run quite as fast, or climb quite as high, or play quite as long. Physical ability was easy to take for granted when you had it.

Phyl stepped on the green jealousy plant in her heart and told Andy, "You'll go every step of the way if we have to carry you."

5
Dig Out
the Root

If the day had been ordered especially for the camp-out, it could not have been more perfect. The sun was bright and the breeze cool. Marty's baby sister sang and cooed happily as she climbed over the laps of the girls in the car.

Andy squeezed her and said, "I'm going to wad you up and put you in my backpack. Then I'll take you home with me."

Gwennie laughed, wrapped her arms around Andy's neck, and then tried to climb into Andy's knapsack.

"Hey," Andy teased, "you're squashing my sandwiches."

Gwen laughed and hugged her again.

Finally the shimmering lake stretched out before them. After the tent was set up, Marty's mother gave last-minute instructions before letting the girls hike out on their own. "Stay on the marked trail; if anyone gets hurt, someone will come along sooner or later. So don't get off the marked path. And be sure to use the rope to help each other up and down. No showing off how good you are without it!"

The girls agreed impatiently. Anything to get going. Then, just as Marty's mother finished, Gwennie attached herself to Andy with a vice grip. She had to be lured away with a cookie before the girls could skip out quietly.

"Is she ever going to be mad when she finds out Andy's gone!" predicted Marty. "I'm glad I won't be around to hear it," she said, demonstrating with her fingers in her ears.

They were barely out of sight when Gwennie's peal of anger and anguish reached them.

"Forget about her," Phyl said. "Let's enjoy

where we're going. Just look at that gorgeous mountain! The day is all ours, and the sun is hardly awake yet. I'll bet we can see forever from the top of that pile of rock!"

Marty pointed to the map. "Here's the stream that marks the beginning. We follow the stream for an inch-and-a-half, so that's a mile-and-a-half; then we go straight up. We can take the rocks or the path."

"I vote for the path," put in Pat.

Andy said nothing. She knew that if she were not along, the girls would scale the rocks like mountain goats.

Marty was reading the warning list. " 'Avoid spiders, lizards, and snakes,' it says. Aw, shucks; I wanted to play with the snakes. 'Racoons, opossums, rabbits, and squirrels inhabit the area, along with deer, bobcats, and other larger game.' Look at this: 'Take care not to disturb the eagles at the summit.' "

"What do they think we are?" Pat asked indignantly. "We've never bothered an eagle in our whole, entire lives."

They had previously decided to rest five minutes every half hour. According to the chart, that would allow them to reach the top of the mountain, spend an hour there, and be back at the lake by sundown.

After the first rest stop, they left the stream and followed the winding path. Andy looked with dread at the straight-up path. She was tired already. Maybe she should have exercised to shape up for the trip. If she didn't use her breath for talking, it might help. She checked her watch for the next rest stop. Fifteen more minutes. Coming down should be a lot easier, she hoped.

At one point Phyl, Marty, and Pat raced away from the path to a cluster of brilliant flowers, so Andy sat down to wait. Rest every minute you can, Andy told herself; it's a long way to the top.

Phyl climbed up every rock she saw and jumped from one to the other, Marty and Pat following.

How do they do it, Andy wondered. I should have stayed in camp and played with Gwennie. No—then they'd have stayed too. I just wish climbing were easier.

Mid-point on the trail they stopped for a snack at some stone tables and benches. The view was magnificent! The lake looked like a puddle left over from a rain shower. The girls decided one of the specks in the puddle was Marty's dad, out fishing.

Back on the trail, the four made a game of joining hands, but Andy knew it was because of her. Why do they do it? she asked herself. How was I lucky enough to have friends like this? They have everything; they don't need me—but I sure need them!

The sun beat down unmercifully as they scaled the last large rock. Phyl was on top first and threw the end of her rope over the ledge to Andy. She hardly had the strength to hold on, so Phyl pulled and the others pushed her to the top. When Andy's head stopped swimming, she looked around. The height made her sick to her stomach, and she sat down suddenly.

"Are you all right, Andy?" Pat asked.

"I'm fine," she lied. "Just resting."

Andy wasn't hungry, but she ate to keep the others from noticing. She tried to keep looking at the ground and not out over the landscape.

Phyl left for a few minutes, then came back and announced, "Let's go down over that way," and she pointed over a cliff.

"Is it a marked trail?" Marty asked.

"No, but we can see the trail from there," Phyl assured them. "Come and look."

Pat and Marty went to the edge and agreed; they could keep their eyes on the markers and join the trail about a half-mile down.

While Marty and Phyl studied the rocks for a new way down, Pat came back and stretched on the ground beside Andy. In a low voice she asked, "Are you going to make it?"

"Sure," she told Pat. To herself she said, Maybe going down won't be easier. What if I fall?

The hike down passed between rocks as big as houses. Eagles could be seen soaring in all directions. Andy climbed awkwardly over one rock and then another. She finally had a chance to rest when Phyl tied the safety rope around a stout sapling, then her waist, and lowered herself into a crevice to examine a nest.

"Three baby birds," she called back. "I'm getting out of here before Mamma comes home!" She climbed hand over fist back up the rope.

After a weary half-mile they reached the trail markers they had seen. But Pat, with a worried

98

look on her face, said, "I don't remember this place."

She was right; nothing looked familiar to any of them.

Marty grabbed the map and spread it on the ground. "I know what happened. This is the rocky trail."

Icy fingers of fear grabbed Andy's heart.

Marty continued, "We can go back to the top and go back down the other path. We'll only lose an hour, and we'll still be off the mountain by sundown."

"But it's so much closer this way," suggested Phyl as she traced the map's rocky trail with her finger.

"But," began Pat, "Andy can't . . . "

"I can make it," Andy cut in. "I'm just fine now. Going down is easy." But she prayed silently, please, Jesus, forgive the lie.

Phyl looked around. "How about it? Shall we?"

Marty and Pat reluctantly agreed. The huge rocks were fascinating, and they all could help Andy. Plus, this trail was a lot more fun. There were caves and ledges, ferns growing in the cracks of the rocks, and springs of water flowing from under some of them.

At a checkpoint Phyl's watch showed them to be much behind schedule. "We're going to have to cut goofing around and get down this hill."

They stretched out single file—Phyl in the lead, then Andy, then Marty and Pat.

They were still quite high when the sun dipped below the tops of the trees. A fear nagged inside each girl, but none spoke of it.

Phyl spotted a shortcut over a rocky ledge and left the path. Andy followed. Phyl jumped neatly over a cleft in the rock and, without hesitation, Andy followed.

Marty screamed, but too late.

Phyl turned just in time to see Andy disappear into the rock. "Andy!" she called into the dark hole. "Are you all right?"

"No, I don't think so."

"What's wrong?"

"I hurt my ankle; I don't think I can get out."

"I'll come down for you," called Phyl. She tied her safety rope to a tree as she had done before and disappeared into the darkness.

Pat and Marty could hear the other two discussing how to get Andy out.

Their plan worked. Phyl tied the rope around Andy's waist, and Pat and Marty pulled her up. Then the rope was let down for Phyl.

When they were both up safely, the sun had set, and the faint light of dusk was around them. They anxiously examined Andy's rapidly swelling ankle.

"I think we should wait for help, like Mother said," decided Marty.

"But we're not on the path," Pat pointed out logically. "She said to stay on a marked trail."

Here was a new problem. Phyl looked at the ankle again and pressed the red part.

"Ouch!" yelled Andy.

Phyl lifted her shirttail to her teeth and tore a strip of cloth. She bound it tightly around the ankle while Andy gritted her teeth in pain.

"Now what are we going to do?"

"Why have to get back on the trail somehow."

"Nice! How?"

"I don't know."

Andy sat silently. Why, oh why did I come? If it weren't for me, they'd be back in camp by now.

Phyl stood up and looked around dejectedly. She thought to herself, my beautiful outing is spoiled. It could have been so perfect. The air, the sun, the rocks, and the mountain. Free, beautiful air. But now we're stuck up here with helpless Andy. Why does she always have to mess things up?

Phyl tried to remember where she had seen the trail marker when she started the shortcut. It had to be close-by somewhere.

"Let's go that way," she pointed. "At least it's closer to the trail, and we can hear someone call."

The others followed dutifully; anything was better than sitting. Andy's ankle bore a little weight when stepping slowly. Marty and Pat walked on either side, helping her when they could.

After a few minutes Phyl finally admitted, "I can't see any markers. We may as well get ready to spend the night up here. I think I saw a shack a few minutes ago. You guys wait here while I check it out. Maybe there's a park ranger or something inside."

"No!" yelled Marty. "We mustn't get separated. Even if we have to stay right here."

"I can follow," Andy promised. "I'm just slow." The pain in her ankle had become blinding stabs of fire when she put weight on it. She held her breath and clenched her teeth as she followed.

"I see it," Phyl called joyfully. "See it outlined against the sky? Even if it's empty, at least it's a roof."

Phyl hadn't counted on the stream between them and the shack. They could hear the sound of rushing water as they approached. There was just barely enough light to see its edge.

Phyl knelt down to examine. "I think there are stepping stones. Whoever made the cabin probably put them there. Let's try it." Phyl stepped bravely on the first stone. "They're covered with moss—and slick," she warned.

A couple stones out, Phyl realized Andy would never make it. Phyl thought, maybe we could find a dry log instead.

She turned to go back just as Andy stepped on the first stone. She saw Andy's wavering motion as she lost her balance. Phyl's mouth opened, but no words came out. She wanted to reach out, but her hand wouldn't move. Her teeth clenched, and her hands clutched each other. Phyl felt as though she were in a dream and every part of her body made of lead.

In the light of the rising moon, Phyl saw the splash and heard the scream as Andy plunged into the water.

In a second Marty also was in the water. "It's not very deep," she called. "Don't worry, Andy; I've got you."

Silence.

Then muffled sobbing. "My arm; I think it's broken."

Phyl forced her hands apart and stepped into the water with Marty. "Which arm?"

"My right."

"Okay," replied Phyl. "Put your left arm around my neck and hold on tight. We're going to wade across. Marty, will you try to steady her without touching her arm? Pat, where are you?"

"Over here," Pat called from the opposite bank. "It's shallow over here, and there's a path."

Phyl and Marty supported Andy as they followed Pat's voice. The night wind was strong, and the girls were shivering as they climbed out of the icy mountain water.

The protection of the abandoned shack was

welcome. They stepped carefully on the creaky floor and found a place for Andy to lie down. The pain of her ankle and arm brought the breath unsteadily to her lungs, and she had not the strength to cry.

Phyl found two lightweight slats and, with strips of cloth from her and Marty's shirttails, bound Andy's arm to make it immobile. "My mother made us all take First Aid," Phyl explained. "We're always having accidents at our house."

Marty went to the doorway and looked out into the darkness. "Somebody should be coming soon. I hope we can hear them; the trail can't be far away."

The mountain silence was punctuated regularly by the screech of an owl and the croak of a bullfrog nearby. Then the wail of a coyote drifted through the trees.

"Those sounds remind me of Andy's recital piece," Phyl decided, " . . . if those animals were instruments, that is."

"Oh, no!" Pat wailed.

"What?"

"Andy won't be playing in her recital—not with a broken arm!"

Silence and the sounds of the animals filled the cabin again.

Andy broke the stillness. "I don't know why you guys do it."

"Do what?"

"Put up with me. I've done nothing but mess up the party all day. Especially Phyl. She had to help me everywhere we went. I should have stayed in camp. I don't know why I can't do stuff as good as the rest of you."

Silence and the animal sounds again.

"I know why," Pat said slowly. "I'm not supposed to tell, but I'm going to anyway. Your mom told my mom, and she told me. When you were born, something happened to make you lose your balance easy and get tired fast. And then your mom couldn't have any more children, either. That's why your mom worries about you and won't let you do much."

Marty turned to Andy. "Well, I don't care! You're part of the club. We need you as much as you need us."

Phyl hugged her knees and shivered in her

wet clothing. You horrible person, she told herself. This is all your fault. You had to hike to Eagle's Nest. You had to come down the wrong trail. You had to take the shortcut. Worst of all, you stood right there and let her fall. But nobody knows that, a thought told her. But *I* know it, her conscience shouted back. She could have drowned, and I'd have been the murderer!

Phyl rose from the floor and walked stiffly through the door. But I've tried. I've honestly tried and tried, God. I don't want to feel this way. Dear Jesus, why don't You take this thought away from me? I keep asking You. Why don't You help me?

The fully risen moon glowed through the trees, flopping ghostly patterns on the ground. Dead leaves rattled as night animals scurried through on their important missions. The bullfrog in the stream had been joined by toads from nearby trees, creating a weird harmony. Phyl's musical ear picked up a vague melody. In the cabin only an occasional sigh punctuated the silence.

Oh, jealousy, how cruel you are! thought Phyl. Andy made the hard climb today with a serious disability, and now she's silently suffering a turned ankle and a broken arm—and she won't

107

even get to play in the recital after weeks and weeks of practice. How's that for bravery? How would she feel if she knew what I did?

Sitting on a rock, Phyl buried her face in her hands. Soundless sobs shook her body.

How do I dig up the root of that jealous weed? It hurts so bad, Lord!

Jealousy is a part of you, Phyl's conscience told herself, and it hurts to lose a part of yourself. Surgery hurts, but when it heals, you'll be well. Suzie was right; God can get inside us and do anything He wants. Jesus, I want that operation right now. Forgive me. And, whenever I start thinking about what other people have, help me think of You and all You've already given me—especially forgiveness.

A sound in the trees caused Phyl to look up, just in time to see the wavering beam of a flashlight.

"Here we are," she called. "Over here!" In a moment she was joined by Pat and Marty, who helped her shout.

Relief caused a shiver from head to toe as Phyl looked into the friendly face of Marty's father. Marty's arms were around his waist, and her face was buried in his chest. Pat was telling him, "Andy's inside. She has a sprained ankle and a broken arm."

The girls led him into the cabin, where he shone his light the full length of Andy. "No bigger than that one is, I can carry her back." With that, he picked her up gingerly and stepped out of the cabin. "There's a path about 20 yards in that direction," he pointed with his elbow, "so we'll go over there. Marty, you shine the flashlight on the ground ahead of me so I don't trip."

Relief gave the girls new strength, and in less than an hour they were safely back in camp at Lake Cathrine. The park ranger gave emergency attention to Andy's arm, and all were asleep when the sun broke through the morning mist.

Back in town, Andy's mother had gathered her into her arms. "Oh, Andrea, why did you try to climb that mountain?"

Andy shook her head silently. *If Mother has to ask, she won't understand anyway.*

Andy was not much help remodeling the clubhouse. The cast made her even more clumsy and incapable than usual, so she mostly watched.

"I can hardly believe it," Marty said to Andy, "them letting you use the cassette for the recital. Wasn't it lucky we made it? And there were no mistakes, either."

"Do you know when you get your new teacher?" Phyl asked.

"Just as soon as I get out of this thing," answered Andy, waving her sling like a chicken flapping its wing.

"I wish you'd hurry," scolded Pat playfully. "Here we've had that four-part arrangement of *God the Creator* for two whole days, and you haven't even learned it. And I'm getting sick and tired of slinging papers on both sides of the street. What do you think this is—some kind of picnic?"

"Patricia!" Andy retorted. "If you don't stop that, I won't let you autograph my cast!"

Pat fell to her knees. "Oh, please, your majesty; anything but that!"

Phyl stood on a chair with a paint brush in her hand and watched as Pat and Andy clowned around. Truly, Jesus' surgery on her heart was healing. It was nice to be well again.